IN OUR NAKEDNESS

For information, contact contact@tetra.house.

ISBN: 978-1-960085-03-0

Cover Design by Mance Felker

Tetra House
Los Angeles, CA

IN OUR NAKEDNESS

Lauren Edwards

PREFACE

There have been felt strokes of the unseen throughout my life, something mystical in the periphery, but let me start by saying that this experience is still very much a mystery to me.

It began in water, salt water, in silence and in darkness. Sensory deprivation which I pursued as a therapeutic tool while recovering from severe health challenges in 2017. The early encounters were varied. Sometimes visual perceptions, sometimes mental impressions, but most often a kind of sensory input in my body. An overwhelming wave of feeling and physical sensation that would encumber my entire being. This typically followed by a loss of control over my motor functions and eventually a withdrawn and disembodied sense of my own personhood. While gradual to start, the experience has escalated and changed shape over time. There have been drawings, visual renderings of faces and of patterns, tones, elaborate physical gesturings. But most commonly, and in the case of what you will find within these pages, words. Lots of words. Entire phrases and sentences stringing themselves together to form a message. A teaching. I would later learn from a mentor to call this channeling. Something nonphysical communicating not only to me, but *through* me.

My role in this work has been as a conduit, a witness, and a scribe. A door through which this orchestra of expression may be heard. I am a student of this teaching as much as any. To this day I'd be lying if I claimed to fully understand it all. What it is that's coming through or where it comes from. But I'm not entirely sure that even matters. The timing feels right. Feels like a coming together as much as it does a pulling apart. My hope is that it will be a light for you. My hope is that we can all lean a little deeper into a place of knowing.

What follows is transcription of channeling sessions that occurred between September 19, 2020 and September 29, 2020. Over the course of these 10 days I was met by what I describe as a kind of persistent "knocking". A dense and heavy presence outside of me making itself known. In an effort to preserve the integrity of the transmission no edits, cuts, or modifications have been made to the original body of writing.

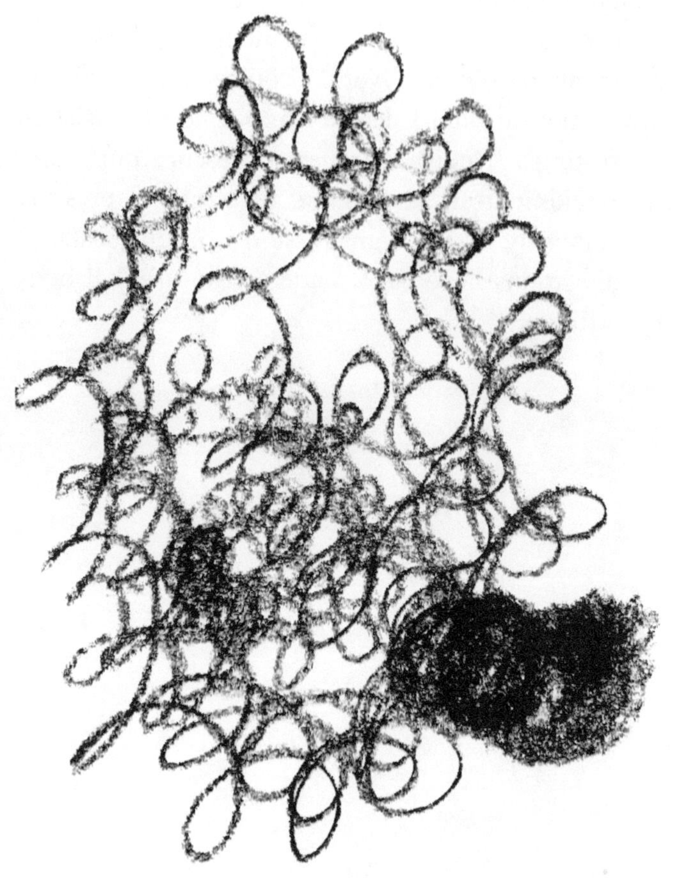

PROLOGUE

The words have been here a long time,
waiting to be written.

It isn't a matter of remembering,
it is feeling, in real time.

> The beginning doesn't so much matter,
> because the beginning is now.

> It is fingers on keys.
> It is a heart, beating.

Do not worry so much
about punctuation or grammar.

What's of substance are the words,
> the ideas,
> being written for the first time.

> Your entire life has been unfolding to this day,
> to this moment.
> Which is the case for everyone.
It's just that, something was lost along the way.
There has been a forgetfulness.

A kind of amnesia that has pulled you so far
from yourselves and your purpose.

> We are here to remind you,
> to be witness to you finding your way back
> home.

What is going to come forward in the following pages has been planned, prepared, carefully awaited for a very long time. You are being asked to be in reception of something entirely new. A different kind of understanding. We wish to prepare you by saying this work is a commitment. Requires incredible focus and time but will change your life and the lives of others forever. You are writing these words because you are ready. Because it is the time. You may be feeling discomfort. In your body, in your energy field. But you will learn to adjust. Learn how to hold it all. Be in rhythm with us as you allow yourself permission to enter the higher room. An elevated frequency.

We begin with one message: This is the time of awakening. Of becoming. Of finding yourselves for the very first time. This is a gift beyond your present comprehension. If you trust, if you allow, you will know.

Be known.

SEPTEMBER 19

2020

There is a knowing in each of you. A kind of navigational system that is guiding you home, steering the ship. The time is here to know your true north. To witness yourselves as what you have always been, but forgotten. The call of the times is one of remembering. *Re-membering*. Putting together again. It is a careful process. One that requires a tremendous amount of certainty that the collective agreements of times passed no longer serve. That new times are necessary.

There is a degree of death to be encountered for new life to be realized and that is the moment in which you find yourselves. Awaiting the new, while still grasping the old. It is an uncomfortable crossroads. It is moving so much of what humanity had long claimed as immovable. And with that, a certain level of shock. A certain rendering of the self as a moment in time. All experience before collapsing, presenting you with the unique experience of yourself free from attachment.

Now, for many, this is met with great difficulty and resistance. And we understand. We know how disorienting it can be to encounter new circumstances that require new ways of thinking, processing, being in the world.

It's a process of reorientation.

It is water moving through stone. Matter you thought was solid but has always been porous. You have the great capacity to adapt, evolve. Be more than you allow yourselves to be. And that is where we meet you. That is the nature of this teaching and what we hope you will soon come to accept as truth. There are many ways, many possibilities. Do not resign yourself to one that is narrow and broken.

Be the light. Feel the call.

September 20

2020

How this is going to be is not what you may anticipate. There is a calling. There is a great rejoicing that many are beginning to listen. We are here beside you, inviting you to know a different way. This begins with the acceptance of a reality beyond what you see here before your eyes. This requires an openness and an understanding that you have so much to learn. Which is an exciting place to find yourself. We hope there is some level of relief in knowing that this, as you know it, isn't it. Isn't everything. We hope there is relief in the promise of something more. And with this in mind, you will begin to find more ease in letting go. Letting go of established notions that have dictated your lives but are so purely human. So malleable. So capable of change. There is a certain degree of trust required moving forward. A trust that the river will carry you, which is a lot more hopeful than clinging on to the rocky shoreline.

The knowingness we speak of is what carries you. Nothing outside, but within. You may think this requires great efforting. May believe that struggle is essential if you want to get anywhere. Let us be very clear, it is not. Not that life is without great teaching that may come in the form of trials or challenges. But this idea that everything is work, that you must tire yourself each day for the promise of a happy life. That is illusion. If you sit with yourself long enough, you will feel this to be true. It doesn't make sense. It is the product of societal programming that has outgrown itself. And what we mean to say is that you are operating from an agenda that is not your own. Not from a feeling space. It is from duty and obligation and the false belief that this is just how things are. To make such a claim is to hold a belief in permanence.

The permanence of anything relies on time. There is constant change, constant motion, independent of you or the ideologies you subscribe to. When we speak of time we do not mean your human understanding of it. A clock, a watch, a calendar. We mean time as a life cycle. Nature makes this easier to grasp. Recurring change - seasons - that may fluctuate, be influenced by external factors, but the inevitable end of one always comes. There is a kind of liberation when you don't hold on too tightly. It is an overinvestment in the material that makes this hard. That is what we wish to speak to you about.

This moment is showing you just how much your lives have been shaped by material conditions. Which is not bad, don't get us wrong. Materiality and material experience is incarnation. Is the foundational purpose of taking a body. But it is not all. When you make it all, there is profound emptiness. Many of you know this. Many of you come to understand this emptiness as a condition. As a state of being. Depression. Anxiety. Loneliness. You give it names, you give it diagnosis, you medicate and try to numb it. You think of yourself as separate and alone. All experiencing varying expressions of the same malady- a disconnect from self. From source. From this internal knowingness that there is more.

Your consciousness exists outside of these paradigms. Outside of these systems and structures that keep you small. Keep you believing that you're a failure or somehow a defective human. There is no such thing. There is no way to be.

———

There is a source for you to know. One you may often feel separate from. Outside of. But it is radiant and it is in you. In your blood, your body, your spirit, and the self beyond what you can conceive of. There are certain limitations imposed on you by your societies, your lineages, your ancestry that condition your understanding of who you are and where you come from. While that serves a purpose and has value in the way of understanding connection, it is a limited framework. It has served in the name of otherness more than it has unity. It has created a false sense of sovereignty and supremacy. False wars, false ideals, false belief in the I and not the We. The binaries of man are so astounding. Must it really be either/or? Must it really be you versus them? Why? What wound is there that has claimed this to be so? We invite you now to consider this. Consider the reasons you might wage yourself against another. Might laugh in the face of kindness, love, acceptance.

Sit with it a moment.

This is your prerogative but it does not make it justified. There is a time when all will see this clearly, each and every single one of you. But for the pain to be mitigated, for there to be greater ease during these transitional times, we come with this offering. You are light. You are the sum total of a universe expanded and collapsed. You have the great authority and power to become yourselves again. To move through the smoke screen and mirrors towards new possibility. It is our hope that through the teaching that follows, you will begin to sense that possibility. Hold it close to you, await the new day.

September 21

2020

Time is in motion. There is now, and there is the way you dictate time as past, present, future. This is helpful for your tracking of patterns, ideas, ways of coexisting. The thing about this understanding is that it condenses something much more layered, much more involved.

We want to give you an example of time as it truly exists. Imagine you are above your body watching yourself go through the motions of everyday life. You have a sense of where you are, and what is going on before you, but they are happening simultaneously. Two different planes within one reality. Time is a measure of multiple dimensions. Time is like an accordion making one sound through compression and motion. There are layers, there is folding. There is the way you see yourself from above and the way you exist below.

When you are in presence, you can more easily interact with the vibration of being.

We know this language may sound abstract but it is the most precise way of comprehending resonance. The time continuum is an expansive sound. It exists as waves, as movement, as feeling. More easily grasped through the body than the mind. It is an exercise to engage with, which may require some time, but we want you to get more comfortable with being in a body and *feeling*. Not just thinking. The mental chatter is what is contributing greatly to this moment you find yourselves in. One of fear, unrest, uncertainty. It is projection of the mind that shapes reality. It is your expectation that there has always been war, so there will continue to be. It is a time of great turmoil for humankind because you've yet to divest from narratives that keep you in scarcity. You receive and listen to the gospels of your peers, your families, your news outlets and believe them to be true so fervently that you completely detach and dissociate from your own knowingness. What you feel in your body. What your instincts tell you. This is where we want to begin.

———

Theoretically, there is more than what meets the eye. You can hold this idea with relative comfort. Call it possibility, call it imagination, call it a summer's day in fall. The illusion is that your eyes are the ultimate truth tellers.

We want you to conceptualize yourself as a light. As something that emits color and frequency. There is a way you can imagine your being as devoid of borders or boundary. There is a way to tap into your felt sense and awareness of yourself outside of parameters. The only focus of this exercise should be your awareness of how you might exist if there were no body. Your essence without form. This is a simple stretch of the imagination that exemplifies a greater truth. That the mind can lead when the body is still. The importance of this having to do with your impetus towards material constructs when the very thing leading you is felt and unseen.

We have a proposition for you. What if you went just one day allowing yourself to be without your own bias and relative understanding of how things work? What if you suspended your judgement and kept a sense of childlike wonder and curiosity about all that is. All that could be? We encourage you to try this — just for fun at first — but then consider how everyday is in fact this way. The myth of the impossible is the byproduct of a civilization that wants to control. Wants to make itself an authority and a ruler of all things. This proclivity was born from man. It's a curious thing, the way you try to codify, label, name what is not yours. This will likely be uncomfortable, because it's all you really know, but this is the work of the time that we are helping usher you towards.

Limited understanding requires limited frameworks and this is what we wish to liberate you from. Who taught you that the way things are are the way they have to be? Have always been? Who taught you that your name is your identity? Your skin is your badge? Who enforces the   ideologies   that   you   summon yourself towards each day? If you cannot name the creator, why do you hold on so tightly? Why do you assign yourselves roles and responsibilities and hierarchical thinking? Why do you get up each day playing someone else's imaginary game? Truly. You are not as subjugated as you think. What you put attention towards is where your life force energy beckons you. It's magnetic. It is creation. You want to rationalize, justify, give away your power. Argue that this isn't so. But you are fooling yourself. Defending a false victimhood. Resigning yourself to being a passive receiver rather than an active creator. This is what must be unlearned. Your allegiance towards suffering is what we must question. Your freedom of being is so much closer than you recognize, allow yourselves to fathom. If there is a moment to know this, it is now. It is the weight of collapse burrowing in your body, the edge of a cliff in front of you, the levees breaking. Great enough force will not be restricted by old rules. We are not saying this is the only way, but it is the most pressing. Is where you find yourselves. There is a certain quality to force that holds its own teaching. You may be feeling more than you have in a long time. Maybe more than you ever have before. You are brushing up against your edges. Learning how to reconcile harm that has gone on for too long. There is an urgency now that wasn't felt before. A call to action. And through that call, you are more open to transformation.

There is a way to be engaged with this that engenders ease and not fear. There is a way to heal your wounds and the wounds of those that came before. This requires aligning to a different frequency. This requires divesting from your old habits and patterning of abuse. We say this carefully, we say this with intention. But it must be named. Your beliefs, whether conscious or not, have normalized abuse. Abuse of the planet, abuse of yourselves, abuse of each other. This has been inherited, this has been normalized, and it must be rectified. The hamster wheel cannot keep spinning. You are tired, you are sick, you are worried all the time. It lives in the body. Is so acutely felt. And yet you continue as if nothing is wrong. Surrender yourself to the abuse because it is what you have known. What you've gone to bed with. Let us be clear, it is not your fault. But it is your inheritance. Yours to dismantle. Some may find themselves moored by this, think it too much, but all of the greatest achievements were one man's idea of too much. We aren't saying it will happen in a day, but we are asking you to imagine if it did. What the world might look like, how you might feel. It is your reason for being to find out.

September 22

2020

There is a functioning of the mind that we want to address, want to bequeath you with. It has to do with the tendency to assume the worst. It is your nature to cling on to fear because the human experience has depended on survival. It is in some ways encoded in your DNA but not entirely necessary. Not useful in the way it once was. Can and should be reprogrammed. The times of fear allowed for you to be here but won't guarantee the continuation of your species. Fear is an idea as much as it is a mechanism. It is the causal factor in much of what you do and much of what motivates you. There is the way you operate from instinct and intuition— true knowingness—and the sensory override that is fear. Think of this very moment. How many of your decisions just in one day were bred from fear? How many of your ideas are warped and distorted because you are afraid? Because you don't want to get sick, or hurt, or feel pain. This is completely reasonable. It is smart and it has kept you alive. What it doesn't serve is your ability to adapt. Your ability to bend and move when faced with new challenges. Fear is immobilizing. It keeps you in smallmindedness and asserts itself as safety. Fear is not safety. It is the illusion of safety while rendering everything you cannot control a threat. There are fewer threats in this world than you believe there to be. You give a mostly benevolent landscape imagination that it does not have. Project your worries and concerns onto others in a way that is infectious. Contagious. And so it goes, one man's fear is like kerosene to an entire community's fire. It spreads and rages and ultimately causes more alarm and danger than was ever really there. Becomes unmanageable. Takes on a life of its own.

The time for transformation is upon you.

There is a way you can approach this from fear, or from possibility. The story of doom and gloom is one that you buy into. One that harms you, but also gets you high. Is addictive. You know togetherness when it is in fear. There is a shared ethos among you that loves to get wound up in your worries and grievances. Loves to complain. Loves to harbour hurt and resentment. None of which *feels* good. But the outcome of which is often some expression of care or understanding. Being validated in your experience.

Feeling less alone.

The opportunity you have now is to shift your awareness elsewhere. Be less attached to your ego projections and more in your knowingness. The way you can begin to unravel from these shared paradigms is through a form of radical awareness. What is really going on before you? What is projection or assumption? What is reigniting an old wound or pattern? Your ability to engage with this as practice will shift your experience dramatically. Offer you new perspective and insight.

There is a certain construct upheld in the collective consciousness of this time that if one suffers, all must. Sometimes in the way of solidarity, sometimes in the way of revenge. But what does it really matter? Either way you are hurting. Either way you are in scarcity or smallness holding yourself to the belief that the world is a scary place. Imagine if we were to subvert that belief system. Imagine if all the energy that is poured into your complaints, your technology, your political agendas, your ways of othering— was reclaimed. You think this isn't possible. But it is. This is the year of not possible being made so. Ask yourself what is gained through holding on to old ideas. Ask yourself where the discomfort stems from. There is such expansive healing available if you are willing to sit with these questions. Sit with yourself in earnest.

The hope is that you will turn away from the poor behavior witnessed in others and take accountability for yourself. Every word you speak against another is energy you give to the very thing you say you are against. Say you will not stand for. How about what you will stand for? How about what matters in your heart? The lessons are so far beyond rigid and binary thinking. So much more illuminating of your individual needs and desires. Your shared humanity.

The reason this is so hard is that you consider yourself other. Somehow separate from the whole. This notion is the byproduct of your togetherness being severed by fear. The template for which greater separation merges with the subconscious. We mean, you internalize without fully realizing what is going on. You operate from something within, a seed of sorts, that was planted but never fully consented to. Now you are amidst the overgrowth of a garden that was never yours to begin with. But you find yourself there, in the thick of it, uncomfortable and afraid. Consumed by old growth that you continue tending to despite the resistance in your body. A feeling that things are not as they should be.

Not as they could be.

If given an empty plot of soil, what seeds might you plant instead?

2020

The hope of man is what's enduring. Hope is the antithesis of fear. Hope is an energy and a frequency that has sustained millenia. Been the primordial force that drives consciousness. Now, hope as you may know it is greatly misunderstood. It is scoffed at, belittled, made to seem naive. As though it is some derivative of an imaginary construct.

Not the case.

Hope is born from uncertainty. Hope is looking out at a barren landscape and finding the part of yourself that chooses possibility over fear. It is active. Conscious. A choice. The way it has been reduced makes it seem inert when it is not. It lives within you. Breathes life into your being. Compels the spirit. When you feel far from fear you may be taking yourself towards a deeper knowingness that you aren't even fully aware of. This knowingness we speak about is like a shadow that requires light to be seen. It is consciousness without form. It is there even when you doubt it and does not sway at the whims of outside influence. It is anchoring. It is the vehicle for forward motion unbound by limitation.

The reason for your knowingness has less to do with you, the individual, and more to do with your common good. When we say this we do not exclusively mean humankind. We mean the planet— we mean nature, we mean animals. You do not show cruelty or disregard when you act from your knowingness. You are kinder, more intentional with your words and with your time. Not so consumed by your ego. The habitual patterning of the small self butts up against your knowingness because there is fear taking charge of your command center. This unconsented to presence that is so futile you cannot begin to imagine another way.

This is where things get interesting.

Your body is as much a channel for good as it is for bad. We do not mean this as a sort of universal polarity but for the sake of your understanding we use these terms. A reframe might be, what is helpful and what is not. There is your knowingness, and there are the slew of external forces, some man made some not, that challenge your knowingness.

To be in alignment with how you feel is to remember the way of water. How you are but a drop in the sea and nothing can change your true nature. You can change and adapt, be influenced and transformed— as the river, as rain, as ice becoming steam. But you are water. You are the thing you know yourself to be. How you organize yourselves has a great deal to do with what shape you take as water. There is the light of the world waiting to name itself as you but first we must dispel some myths.

You are not just a body, you are not

just your thoughts, you are no one else's projected idea of you. You are the illumination of consciousness in form and structure. You are profoundly unique and yet profoundly unaware. Which makes this kind of fun in a way. There is so much to be discovered. So much play to be had. The time is now and if you've found yourself stumbling across these words you are closer than you think. To deeper truths, to your knowingness.

———

How might you engage with yourself if you were to be unconcerned with the perception of others? Both inwardly and outwardly. Less involved with doing and more involved with the ways of being that require feeling. It is something this generation in particular is so removed from. Again, this is no fault of your own. These words do not come as punishment or retribution. They come as an offering. They come as guidance during difficult times. For you to sit with and imagine the prospect of more. How you feel is paramount to what you think, what is told to you by your governments or authority figures. How you feel is a compass unto itself. A guidepost for living with integrity and alignment.

It is one of the big mistakes of this time to suppress feeling. To grin and put on a happy face when you are hurting. To lie— for the sake of a job, a relationship, a principle, or a duty. Because where does the truth go when it is not heeded? It festers in the body. It builds and builds, compresses and compounds until the suffering can no longer be held. This is paramount to nearly every other condition. Of the body, or the mind. Because it is the origin. Source of so many diseases and ailments that you do not give credence to. The harmony of your being relies on expression. Relies on your ability to engage with and process what you are feeling. Certain traumas are established because feeling is regarded as a subsidiary experience. That it does not affect humanity on a deeply integrative level. The compulsion to repress feeling is a form of Authoritarianism. It is nuanced and is how so many people wake up each day in a catatonic state of compliance. The will is being trampled. The spirit is dim and detached from itself. You must pay mind to your tendency to accept what is harming you. We say this with great compassion, but awareness is necessary. There are fear tactics employed in nearly every area of your life for why you should not divest from the ordinances laid before you. Institutions, the status quo. There are rules for existing that are entirely made up but have you in agreeance.

There is more autonomy than you believe there to be. More agency in shaping your reality. For the betterment of yourself and others. The only concern that is pertinent for the healing of the collective has to do with your ability to evaluate emotionality and the deep intelligence that comes from feeling.

You say— what about famine, what about war, what about the great atrocities happening concurrently each day? Well, they have a source. Large scale global crises does not appear overnight. We are talking about decades upon decades of detachment and fear. We are talking about a century's worth of problems coming to the surface when the original wound was never tended to. Now there are many historical cycles that have shaped the trajectory of humankind— but we are talking specifically about what has led you here. To this moment of reckoning. There is this way you often mistake your own experiences as independent of others, but you are so much more tangled up than you could possibly fathom. Your suffering is another's suffering. How you are feeling at any moment projects to those around you and creates a ripple effect in frequency. We mean quite literally. This is not to say be happy all the time. That in itself is a construct to invalidate the spectrum of feeling that is vital to the human experience. We are however saying, performative behavior bred from repressed and unexpressed emotion is a detriment to all. It is dishonest and it is how your hurt grows to be so blatantly brash. How you see yourselves as somehow fooling others is so completely misguided. There are these faulty perceptions about being self sufficient, not relying on anyone else. But this way of pretending is so completely untrue. How do you eat? How do you wash your hands? How do you find a place and call it home? No one is outside of the collective ecosystem, even if you attempt to be. This meaning that there is a kind of symbiosis that you participate in each day whether you are aware of it or not. Self reliance is not the way of your knowingness— you need others.

How you respond to help or care is more a reflection of your wounding than it is any mark of strength or dignity. The purpose of calling attention to this is so that you may begin to understand the forces at play when you think of yourself as some anomaly witnessing everyone else go about their lives. It is the call of the planet to assign greater reminders that you are not alone. Not as separate as you may feel in this moment.

2020

To every word there is an energy and a quality. The transmission of words are like poems of the subconscious. No matter how you filter yourself, you take words into your being. The reason we bring this up has to do with your willingness to be of a new mindset. Consider the words you allow into your psyche. Consider the way you speak to yourself and others. Consider what you read in media, what you listen to, whose words you allow to permeate your energy field. Are you thinking for yourself? From your knowingness? Or are you operating from a place of reactivity in response to what is told to you?

There is a quality of mindfulness that we wish to teach you. This is a technique for you to try when you are overloaded with information and begin to feel yourself grow overwhelmed by thought. Hold a picture of yourself in front of you. Look at the person there. Look at their eyes. Look at their face, look at the way they embody space. Hold this image in your mind's eye. With eyes closed, imagine there were a new way of feeling outside the limits you know for yourself. Outside of the time restrictions set forth by others. What if you could open your eyes and not see a representation of yourself but the fullness of who you are in alignment with your knowingness? This exercise is intended for the mind to dissociate itself from projections. There is a difference between visualization and projection. Projection holds attachment to words you've been told. Concepts and ideas that dictate your way of thinking of yourself and of the world. You may say — "Of course, how else would we organize and make sense of our experiences?".

That is what we are trying to demonstrate.

There is a usefulness to words when they come from a feeling space. A creative place. One that is imbued with vision and potential. There is little usefulness to words that are recurring microprograms. You may not see it as such, but the collective mind has a tendency to loop itself. How many times have you heard the same narratives said over and over that you start to believe them as truth? How many times have you found yourself questioning your feelings because they appear to be incongruent to what is being portrayed by your sphere of influence? This might be your family, your workplace, your social media outlets. Each of you is plugged in, in your own way. There is incredible power and value to the hive mind but you can also lose yourself in it when you are not truly listening or in conscious observation of your own feeling.

The problem with the belief in a "higher power" is that you absolve yourself of responsibility to each other. There is so much more beyond this, as we have stated, but it is not hierarchical. It is not an authority dictating your lives. You have conscious choice. You have just as much say in your creation as you do your destruction. You have the potential to become the seeds of new and abundant life. Not to be concerned with the old, but with the new. How you meet this idea holds great importance. The figurative model for this is the bee hive. The queen is the ultimate authority while the other bees work in synchronized flow and find the pollen. How the worker bees operate is in response to the needs of the hive, but each have their own knowingness. They are self motivated, but their commitment is to each other and to the survival of their queen. Humans tend to think of this as hierarchy, but it is not. It is collectivism through the formation of perfect predilection. The queen is your collective mind. Not a singular entity but the product of a colony working in communion. The anatomy of the bee is equal parts idea, equal parts motion. The idea being what it is in service to, motion being the driving force. Your ideas are your words, your motion is your knowingness.

How most are functioning in this moment is from the idea of fear. It manifests as your words and then is internalized in the body. You may feel immobilized, tired, worn down. You may not know how to connect or be in relationship with others outside of talking about fear because it is the most palpable expression of belonging in this moment. The tendency to deny hope is that it feels outside of this shared experience of being together in suffering. The weight of your collective agreements influences so much of how you relate to one another and to yourselves. The paradigm shift that is necessary for the betterment of all starts with naming what beliefs you've adopted out of fear and what feelings you have repressed on account of your beliefs. The way to shift thought is to be more present and aware of what activates in your body when certain words are spoken. What triggers a physical, and therein— energetic, reaction that is uncomfortable? How you move in relationship to words is a dance of the mind meeting the spirit. The harder you try to ignore your feeling, the more you recoil towards the weight of brooding.

The worries come quickly when you are not of your own knowingness. When thoughts engender your behavior towards others, because you are criticizing, rather than creating. There is so much momentum towards your own individual sound boards but they are all emitting the same frequencies. To be in your knowingness is to allow yourself to feel more fully. To not mistake what is yours with what is someone else's. That is what you are not fully conscious to. The words of your enemy are often transmitted and met by you in equal measure. The oppressor and the oppressed are boxes that you create. Finding your center and your knowingness are essential for reordering. For releasing the boxes that keep you small and remembering who you really are.

It is imperative that you do not attach your worth to historical measures. You are liberated from the limitation of those that came before you. You carry their memory, their wisdom, their heritage. But you do not need to carry their pain. You may set it down. You may allow yourself to feel peace and create a future that is on your own terms. From knowingness. To hold on to old pain is to cosign the abuse. Allow it to carry on past its time. This holding pattern perpetuates further pain. Begets a new evolution of something that could be put to rest. Your job is to determine what is yours to carry and what is only occupying precious space.

Figments of actual truth reside in your inherited biome. Words as they are spoken by trees, by plants, by the things that grew long before you got here. You are so small. Not to say insignificant, not to say unimportant or without purpose. But you do not rule this thing!

You are one part. One fractal of a cosmic consciousness. Humble yourselves. Fall to your knees if you must. Tire yourselves so thoroughly that you cannot go on without asking for help. The ego is such a gatekeeper to your sense of solidarity. Ego is the formation of your inner authority imposing a tax

on your knowingness. That to be seen—
to be known in truth and fullness you
must first pay and make others pay for
the right to exist. It is incredulous. It
is the outcome of conditioning and a
mindset that must be challenged.

How you are with the time you're given
can be of great healing or of great
consequence. Only you, and you alone,
can choose to interrupt the trajectory
you are on. Choose what you are in
agreeance to and what you refuse to
accept.

There is hopefulness. There is light.

Now is a critical moment. Your
willingness to engage with yourselves
more honestly will determine many
future outcomes. Your service to
systems that are broken or corrupt
will become glaringly apparent. There
should be no shame in confronting
this. It is happening for all of you in

different ways and is how you will come to know each other more fully. No one is the saint. No one is the righteous one. You are all learning, growing, waking up. We do not punish and you should not either. It is unconstructive and it is punitive of the human condition. There are ways to bend without being so critical of yourselves and others. This is transformation. You are only prolonging your dissatisfaction the more vested you are in retribution. The more you place blame on others. It is immensely unhelpful to complain all of the time. Save yourself the energy. Try finding what it is that makes this life worth living. Try remembering what came before you were told, "this is the way it is". You might as well make it up. That serves you just as well in the face of this moment. We wish to drive home your power, we wish to drive home your purpose, we wish to drive home your connectedness to all things. You are not through being a human. Marinate in the possibility of what could be instead. This is your way of reclaiming yourself.

September 25

2020

Taking the word from your mind to your heart is the practical way of beginning. There is less involved with this than you may think. The most important aspect being how you feel. There is a time for you to be in reception of this teaching as energy and that involves your participation from a heart space. It is a practice if this kind of language is new to you. But it is simple and it is easily learned. Try imagining you are in a car going towards the ocean. You begin to smell salt, seabreeze, and feel a particular quality in the air before reaching the full body of water. Your heart space leading you is kind of like that. Noticing the subtle cues of your sensing body before anything else is perceived. How you are able to conceptualize feeling as a secondary sense but it actually informs your experience, first. Is what leads you, alerts your thinking mind, offers perception. There is a level of trust required when you lead from the heart. Trust in your knowingness. Trust that what you feel is an indicator of something more. Something greater. The tendency to dismiss feeling is to smell fire and disregard the immediate likeliness that something is burning. That you could be in danger. That someone might need help.

Most of humanity at this time is walking around ignoring the smell of fire.

There is a knowingness there that may be tapped into at any moment. A precise tool that can cut through the triple threat of ideas, conditioning, and doubt that cloud your judgement. This is not a how-to instruction manual, it is more a reasoning for your own self advocacy. A reasoning for your being outside of established thought patterns or rules. There are no rules. You make them up. Anything you hold in high esteem as authority or law, you made up. Anything that dictates behavior outside of feeling is part of systemic patterning that someone at some point made up. Feels a bit bonkers to wake up each day and continue operating a machine that was not made for this time. To hold yourself accountable to rules that are old and decaying. To power structures that hurt you and hurt the planet. The great deception is making you believe that you can't live otherwise. That there isn't hope. That you must wither up under the iron fist of your fear and be these fractured versions of yourselves.

No!

Let us say it again— no, no, no.

There is more for you. All of you. There is beauty, there is love, there is perfect and divine order when there is feeling. You may struggle with this if you were ever punished for feeling. It might have planted doubt in yourself and your knowingness. But this is the redemptive beauty of this moment allowing you to see yourself more fully, allowing you to reclaim agency over your life and divest from toxic ways of thinking that martyr your ability to thrive. Finding a way out is your collective task. It is a unified effort of the self in agreement with others. It will take many forms, many iterations, so do not concern yourself with how others choose to behave. A strict adherence to one set of principles does not serve everyone. Allow others some grace. Allow yourself to be humbled by the goodness of your kind if you pause for just one moment. If you lean into feeling. If you let the river take its course.

Your service to each other may not take the form you think. You cannot heal by not first looking at the wound. There is a requirement for awareness. There is a requirement for accountability. There is a requirement for you to get honest with yourself and see how your hurt may have been misplaced onto another. This is not easy, this is not fun, but it is necessary. It is essential for this growth cycle. It is emptying out the bag you otherwise kept shut. It is not your job to solve the world's "problems", but it is your job to name how you participate in them and course correct. There is such great disconnect with the self. Whether through projection, narcissism, dissociation, disembodiment. These are all varying expressions of the same thing. You cannot be conscious towards any cause if you are not first sitting with yourself. The final passageway towards a new understanding has only one person standing guard and that is you.

2020

Following your feeling towards the path of knowingness is like being on a ride where you cannot see what's before you. There is the place you find yourself and there is the weight of something propelling you forward. When you are trying so hard to be in flow with your own sense of the collective agreements you keep yourself from experiencing where the ride might take you.

To be in rhythm with the foundational truth of knowingness is to surrender your limited perception of control. Which is funny because your tethering to so-called "truths" are actually untruths controlling your sense of what is real and what is not. You are afraid not to know and so you accept what has been placed before you as the infallible and the bereft. Finding your own way through the illusion is a matter of feeling more than you think, listening more than you interject, and holding a mirror to yourself before you pass judgement on another. The greatest gift you can offer yourself is this. The greatest achievement of your life will come if you are not so resistant to the greater unfolding.

How you show up to this occasion is a new way of being. It is synchronistic. It is without the harmful binary understandings that have clouded so much of how you relate to yourselves and what it means to be conscious. You are in the process of unraveling. Coming undone. Forgetting your ways of balancing disparate thought and integrating in new formation. The visual of a starburst is helpful here. You are one solar ray of a much larger light force. You are able to emanate light that extends beyond where the source is located. You are able to break away from the most known fire and become your own light in the dark. We do not wish to confuse you— this is not individualism. This is collective knowingness. Finding the light within you is finding it in another. This is a form of being that is

through and for the greater good. This is
alchemy. This is a transcendence of the
mind through the heart.

This language may unsettle some of
you— we acknowledge that. But take a
moment to consider the language you
so readily adopt and accept as truth.
Do you question the authority of your
doctors, your politicians, your "experts"?
Those who may hold good intentions
but are so plugged in to a broken
system that they've forgotten their own
knowingness. It is not a moral question
of who is right and who is wrong, it
is awakening towards a new sun. It is
being willing to sit with the darkness
long enough that you realize you are
cold, and tired, and wish to see. How
this happens is gradual but so much
more accessible than you even realize. It
is the form before the conscious arrival.
It is motion and it is movement and it
is happening right this moment. If you
are feeling grief, if you are feeling fear,
if you are feeling anger or rage you are
actually much closer than you know.
The question we want to put forth
is— where are you operating from? The

place of grief, fear, anger, rage? These are important expressions of feeling. They are dense and they are motivating. But they are not all. They are surface to a greater expanse of feeling. Of knowing. Of closeness with yourself.

Do not try and sabotage your feeling by believing that truth is somehow outside of you. It is you. You are here because you are truth. You are here because the remembering requires you to be so. There is no exception or exclusion. There is no picking favorites. How you may be inclined to defend your own judgement is peril onto the self. It is false and it is arrogant. It is assuming that you hold a benefit that others do not. No one's knowingness is superior or more prestigious. It's just a matter of how far along you are in your learning. Who you had in the way of mentors, helpers, guides. Who taught you what you know. Be it good or be it the basis for misunderstanding. There is a lot to undo here. We are certain you gather that by now. But at what cost? You are the holders of these keys. You are the hope and the creators of a different reality. We bow to you in reverence because it is no small feat. It is completely new and it is the first time for you to be truly alive.

Here's to living.

2020

For there to be a knowing there must also be a memory of how to access it. The idea that you were born from nothing is nice and easy to accept but it is not the full expression. You are a seed. You hold the memory of everything that came before and the potential for everything that comes after. There is no playing small once you are able to fully grasp this idea. There is only remembering and becoming.

How is it that your own sense of what is possible tarnishes the very thing that is keeping you alive? We mean the mental limitations imposed by your conditioning dictate your limitless nature. There is only so much we can say to drive this point home. Your mental frameworks get in the way too easily. What we suggest is trying to exercise this by allowing yourself to be in greater observation. To pay closer attention to the truisms and processes people around you hold themselves to unabashedly. Then question the origin of those behaviors and beliefs. If they can be learned, they can be unlearned. Neural networks can be re-formed. Things begin to change once you are shown that something better is possible. There is no one and only path. Do not resign yourselves to someone else's diagnosis when you aren't really sick— just uncertain, just lost, just out of touch with your knowingness. You give so much of your power away. When you begin to engage more in a sensing way you will come to see this clearly. You will come to see how many of your reactions are patterns, your ideas are regurgitated, and much of what you speak is from fear and limitation. Once you begin to illuminate these things as an observer you bring conscious awareness to them. It requires humility and the ability to step outside your ego, but there is so much more to be experienced if you can do this. You are getting unstuck. You are merging worlds. There is no guarantee that it will be easy, but it will be real. The outcome of incredible resilience and bravery.

How this is done is up to you.

There is the way of water, and there is the way of resistance. You may hold on for as long as you'd like but the more inflexible you are the more discomfort you will encounter as things start to change around you. There is no sense in this when there is levity and ease waiting for you on the other side. How you participate in the refocusing of your energy is key to unlocking a greater depth of your knowing.

The hypocrisy of these times at present is in the way you expect a different outcome by way of the same behaviors. Same rules. Same oppressive systems. How is this a problem to be solved by limitation? It's not. It is the future correcting the past. That is how you must see it. It's forward time creating the moment in which you stand. Your best, most creative self reaching backwards to help you along. Holding you in perfect guidance. There is a degree of imagination required. Because imagination activates a part of you that has been stunted by your falsehoods. The wonderful thing about your imagination is that it is not prisoner to the limitations set forth otherwise. How you begin to open yourself up to possibility is the most influential thing that can be accessed in the way of your collective future. Finding the right modalities for your vision is the fun part. You each are so gifted in divine but different ways. Each of you is an essential building block to the composite whole. We don't say this lightly. There is an ecosystem that you depend on and that depends on you. Your ability to sift through all the noise and find your own sound is what we are talking about. Before anyone told you what you are capable of. Before anyone else decided for you. It seems almost unfathomable. But there is an origin that existed before all the rules. There is a depth of knowing that is far more wise than any singular somebody who called themself a teacher, doctor, priest, parent.

Allow yourself to feel the enormity of that.

Allow yourself to be free from an identity that was dictated for you. The path is yours. The path is not predetermined by anyone with a badge or a degree or a fancy nameplate.

It is co-created.

One by one in perfect pitch.

The final teaching we wish to impart is one of frequency. There is no world without it. Every cell in your body moves in frequency. Every word you speak is spoken in frequency. Every color, every sound, every emotion, every thing. This is something we want you to grasp fully. A lesson in vibration and resonance. When we speak about energy, about feeling, this is not conceptual. This is quite literal in the mode of frequency. The field of study that has propelled this forward is Quantum Mechanics. For those of you that need science to validate your experience, the science is there. It is young and it is focused but it is rendering much of what the old world already knew.

There is a certain kind of supremacy you hold over your ancestors as if they were all vagrant mules who knew less than you know now. This is quite rude and is frankly why you've found yourself sideways in your suffering. You may have evolved from a different way of being, but you are not better. You are spokes on the same wheel. The thought that you are among the greatest achievements of humankind isn't entirely true. There were advanced civilizations that came before you that were deeply connected to the unseen. There may not be much in the way of material record, but do not fool yourselves into thinking this is the pinnacle of existence. It is not.

Time is nonlinear, but if you wish to think in terms of a historical timeline, you have barely been born. Your kind has taken many strides in different directions since the beginning. Looked for meaning and fulfillment in many different places. Some of which have gotten the better of you. But now is about integration. Now is about bridging old wisdom with new resource. Now is about stripping away the broken processes that were built to control and becoming who you were intended to be. A new spoke in the wheel. There is so much you can learn if you loosen your grasp. There is so much in the way of collective healing and liberation if you are able to concede that you do not know everything.

How you are with each other is a good place to start. We speak of frequency because each of you emits a kind of wavelength. Conceptualize this as your energy body. You are constantly interacting with each other in frequency even when your mouth is shut, your eyes are closed, or your physical body is separate. This is so crucial for you to get. You are emitting and receiving nonstop. You are walking energy towers that share an energetic field.

When the frequency is fear, that has the ability to pulse through all of you. When the frequency is love, the same applies. We are not saying it is one or the other, we are not saying this is euphoria. We are saying that mindful awareness of what you are taking in and what you are putting out is absolutely necessary. With the way you've come to wield technology, this energy network has been rapidly altered. You are more connected in some ways, but disconnected in those that matter most for your survival.

It is easy for the frequency of greed, fear, scarcity, doom to travel and snowball. It activates a biological response in you that then permeates the air and colors every interaction that you have with others. This can be repressed, numbed with substances or other coping strategies, but the frequencies are continuous until they are interrupted. This is where we circle back around to your knowing, your feeling, your guided sense of what is and what isn't. Holding yourself to a standard that emerged from fear is of no service to the collective mind. Every individual plays a part in the manifestation of what comes next. You think yourselves to be so separate. You think of walls, borders, divisions, but these are all occupying the same frequency of consciousness. If you are asking how you can be aligned to a different frequency, we want you to think of a clock. The analog kind with marked minutes and seconds. If you follow the hand around once you will just have spent a minute in present observation. You will have slowed the mind enough to focus intently on what is before you and only that. Only aware of what is occurring in real time. There is an urgency in your wavelength when you operate outside of presence. Things begin to feel dire or insurmountable when, most often, they are not. Not as severe or life-threatening as they register to be.

Notice how you feel in your body before and after you engage with others. Notice how you feel when you are silent and alone versus when you are activated by something you read, something you saw, or something you heard. Reactionary patterning has become your defaulted way of existing. You cling on to frequencies that are shuffling around your shared field and embody them. This comes at great cost. To your health, to your body, to your sanity. Your nervous system is being constantly bombarded with information that envelops and betrays your knowing. That plucks you from yourself and tosses you into the circus of scarcity and survival. It's hard to find joy when the frequency of your shared belief systems leans towards fear and ripples outward in ways unseen.

Feel your heart, the way it beats. There's something to remember here.

September 28

2020

Finding your frame of reference for understanding this teaching is something we want to acknowledge. You are each processing through your individual soul's requirements. This is no minor task. You are in the process of great realization and there are growth edges. There are trials. There are focal points for each of you.

When you ask— "What can I do? How do we fix this?", there has to be an honoring of yourself. You must take into consideration what has been harmed or continues to harm you. You must look for the moments when you seek someone or something to blame before centering the healing that could occur if you allowed an honest expression of your feeling. There is no experience of the self that is not mirrored by the collective. You mustn't be afraid to witness yourself fully. You mustn't be ashamed of the things you did out of necessity or survival or because you were not yet aware that other options were available to you. Believe in reconciliation. Believe that you are exactly where you are because you chose to be. This will allow you to take your power back. This will allow you to tap into your knowingness more authentically without the buffer of your wounding.

There is no hope without your involvement in it.

For you to know yourself in a deeper way, know each other without pretense or preestablished imposition, you will be required to take a seat at the table. You will not have the convenience of someone else's rules. How liberating— but also entirely free from the structures that have given you a safe understanding of what it means to be a human being. There's a lot to reconcile between the circuitry of your sturdy symbiotics. For now, you only need to concern yourself with feeling. Becoming more conscious of your patterning and where in your life you have grown rigid.

2020

The purpose of this teaching is multifold. You owe yourself such an incredible amount of forgiveness. We honor your willingness to come this far, to even consider the hope of a new paradigm. The focus of ours is to endow you with your own resource, your own fortitude, your precious life that has been dimmed by tools of oppression. You think of this concept in limited purview. Think of your shared humanity— that is being oppressed. Limited. Held in smallness. The only thing for you to imagine now is the potential of your being. That in time there will be great change, that you will look back and wonder why you did not trust your knowingness with greater worth.

Finding a positive outlet or expression is a fine place to start. The world's problems will not be solved by means you have been taught. It will require a return to yourself outside of external influence. If you turn off your television, your radio, all of the other ways you are plugged in to constructed out-picturings of reality— what's left? What's being said from inside? It's wrong to think it is empty in there. You've just been impressed and encoded by something louder. How you move forward is up to you. There are great teachings to be found in any decision. It is just our sacred obligation to remind you that there are decisions. You make them everyday. You are making one right now as you read these words. Lauren made one when she decided to listen and bring forth her own knowingness in delivering this message. There is incredible possibility. We will say that again and again until it is realized. You are subservient to false masters and false idols. You are all varying expressions of the same currency. Understand this please. Understand your place is among many and the lie that you are small, that you are undeserving, that you are broken, that you are somehow defective.

This. Is. A. Lie.

You are carrying around the weight of many lies. Some told to you by people you respect, some you created for yourself. They are heavy. They are not worth holding when you could be illumined instead. This isn't pretty language for storybooks. This is truth you have denied yourself. And the consequence of this denial is what you are seeing play out now on a global scale. The forgetting has gone on for too long. Grown destructive and repugnant. Why hold on to what is causing harm? Ask yourselves this. Why continue to suffer? When you trail the question long enough you will find that there is emptiness. There is a hollow void that has been stuffed with things, obstructed from light. Memories have been warped, ideals have been raised, and you've constructed a life out of hollowness. There has been truth in moments. Knowingness that comes in waves. But you filter it. Think it must be coincidence or chance. There is no thing. There is only knowingness and how it is obscured.

Thank you for your willingness to engage with this teaching. Thank you

Lauren for your commitment of time
and energy to be of service to a greater
calling. We are with you all as you are
with yourselves.

Hope is a horizon.

www.ingramcontent.com/pod-product-compliance
Lightning Source LLC
Chambersburg PA
CBHW021344060726
47591CB00006B/2146